Acting Edition

The Identical Same Temptation

by Bob Glaudini

Copyright © 2008 by Bob Glaudini
All Rights Reserved

IDENTICAL SAME TEMPTATION is fully protected under the copyright laws of the United States of America, the British Commonwealth, including Canada, and all member countries of the Berne Convention for the Protection of Literary and Artistic Works, the Universal Copyright Convention, and/or the World Trade Organization conforming to the Agreement on Trade Related Aspects of Intellectual Property Rights. All rights, including professional and amateur stage productions, recitation, lecturing, public reading, motion picture, radio broadcasting, television, online/digital production, and the rights of translation into foreign languages are strictly reserved.

ISBN 978-0-573-66274-4

www.concordtheatricals.com
www.concordtheatricals.co.uk

FOR PRODUCTION INQUIRIES

UNITED STATES AND CANADA
info@concordtheatricals.com
1-866-979-0447

UNITED KINGDOM AND EUROPE
licensing@concordtheatricals.co.uk
020-7054-7298

Each title is subject to availability from Concord Theatricals Corp., depending upon country of performance. Please be aware that *IDENTICAL SAME TEMPTAITON* may not be licensed by Concord Theatricals Corp. in your territory. Professional and amateur producers should contact the nearest Concord Theatricals Corp. office or licensing partner to verify availability.

CAUTION: Professional and amateur producers are hereby warned that *IDENTICAL SAME TEMPTATION* is subject to a licensing fee. The purchase, renting, lending or use of this book does not constitute a license to perform this title(s), which license must be obtained from Concord Theatricals Corp. prior to any performance. Performance of this title(s) without a license is a violation of federal law and may subject the producer and/or presenter of such performances to civil penalties. Both amateurs and professionals considering a production are strongly advised to apply to the appropriate agent before starting rehearsals, advertising, or booking a theatre. A licensing fee must be paid whether the title(s) is presented for charity or gain and whether or not admission is charged. Professional/Stock licensing fees are quoted upon application to Concord Theatricals Corp.

This work is published by Samuel French, an imprint of Concord Theatricals Corp.

No one shall make any changes in this title(s) for the purpose of production. No part of this book may be reproduced, stored in a retrieval system, scanned, uploaded, or transmitted in any form, by any means, now known or yet to be invented, including mechanical, electronic, digital, photocopying, recording, videotaping, or otherwise, without the prior written permission of the publisher. No one shall share this title(s), or any part of this title(s), through any social media or file hosting websites.

For all inquiries regarding motion picture, television, online/digital and other media rights, please contact Concord Theatricals Corp.

MUSIC AND THIRD-PARTY MATERIALS USE NOTE

Licensees are solely responsible for obtaining formal written permission from copyright owners to use copyrighted music and/or other copyrighted third-party materials (e.g., artworks, logos) in the performance of this play and are strongly cautioned to do so. If no such permission is obtained by the licensee, then the licensee must use only original music and materials that the licensee owns and controls. Licensees are solely responsible and liable for clearances of all third-party copyrighted materials, including without limitation music, and shall indemnify the copyright owners of the play(s) and their licensing agent, Concord Theatricals Corp., against any costs, expenses, losses and liabilities arising from the use of such copyrighted third-party materials by licensees. For music, please contact the appropriate music licensing authority in your territory for the rights to any incidental music.

IMPORTANT BILLING AND CREDIT REQUIREMENTS

If you have obtained performance rights to this title, please refer to your licensing agreement for important billing and credit requirements.

THE IDENTICAL SAME TEMPTATION was originally produced at Theater for the New City. It opened on September 18, 2003, and was directed by Bob Glaudini.

The original cast featured:

IDA . . . . Rebecka Ray
MONNIE . . . . Roberta Wallach
TERRENCE/KENT . . . . Sidney Williams

CHARACTERS

IDA .... A nurse; likes passive men.
MONNIE .... Her best friend. A court recorder, prefers aggressive men.
TERRENCE ....Extremely reticent, Ida's most current boyfriend.
KENT................... Terrence's twin brother, raised in England, a forceful personality.

Terrence and Kent are played by the same actor.

TIME

August.

PLACE

New York City.

SET

A studio apartment that serves as both Ida and Monnie's apartments. They are practically identical.

Other areas:

Exterior entrance to Ida's building.

Hospital cafe; a table, chairs.

Courthouse patio; a bench

AUTHOR'S NOTE

Performed without an intermission.

Scene 1

(IDA's studio apartment. IDA, in a robe and furry slippers, and MONNIE, wearing a jacket and clutching a purse, look at TERRENCE, who is on the bed in his crummy underwear.)

IDA. She's my friend, Monnie, I wanted you to meet. My friend, Monnie, I told you about.

(beat)

Well? Say hello, say hello to Monnie.

(beat)

He's passive.

MONNIE. It's OK.

IDA. Tell her how we met, Terrence.

(pause) You felt me staring at you, right?

(pause) Isn't that right? You felt me staring? Terrence? You felt me staring, didn't you? It's OK to tell Monnie! We tell each other everything.

MONNIE. *(pause)* She told me she met someone.

IDA. You felt me staring at you, right, Terrence? Didn't you? In the book store?

(pause) Terrence, didn't you feel me staring?

TERRENCE. Yeah.

MONNIE. You've been together how long already…?

IDA. Since Friday.

MONNIE. The whole weekend?

IDA. Uh-huh, yeah.

MONNIE. It's serious then?

IDA. Stop it.

(beat)

He never says anything on his own initiative.

MONNIE. Is that true? Is it? Is it true, you're the quiet type?

(*brief pause*)

What's his name?

IDA. Terrence.

MONNIE. Is it true, Terrence, you never speak? Never speak unless spoken to?

TERRENCE. If I've something to say.

IDA. He curls up and purrs until you need him.

MONNIE. He's a little kitty?

IDA. It's perfect because he just lies there and you have your way with him. Do whatever you want.

MONNIE. You aren't passive aggressive are you?

TERRENCE. I don't know.

IDA. I'll bet he's excited right now. Two women paying this attention. He's a good boy. He doesn't even drink coffee. Doesn't touch alcohol or smoke. Has a sweet tooth though. Naughty little sweet tooth.

(**IDA** *rubs his stomach.*)

A little pudgy baby Buddha belly.

TERRENCE. Come on...

IDA. Oh.

(**IDA** *rubs his crotch.*)

What's this? Take a feel. You'll see. He looks like he is all uninvolved, but just feel right here. His love muscle will get so hard.

MONNIE. I think I'll pass.

IDA. Very impressive. You're sure?

MONNIE. No offense.

IDA. Well, he's not going anywhere just yet. Are you? Little kitty isn't going, is he? Is he, Terrence?

TERRENCE. No.

IDA. We met when I ran in the bookstore to get out of the rain. Some storm, Friday, wasn't it?

MONNIE. It was *scary*. All the thunder and the lightning.

IDA. I ran into the store, there was a woman reading poetry, I thought, God, I'm in hell. This tiny body on giant platforms. This white flour face, little dark curls dyed yellow at the tips, y'know, and those stupid glasses we hate, and these little, thin, bright red lips. This *I'm so serious look on* her face, reading in a little quiet whisper voice about her vagina, and her mother, and she ended everything screaming – from a little whisper *victim* voice to a horrible screaming. Vagina this, God, vagina, vagina that, and her mother this, her mother that. I fucking started to run fucking right back out! But that's when I saw my little pussy cat sitting at a table in the corner, all wet, staring out the window at the rain, so depressed looking, so "I don't care one way or the other," so helpless looking.

(beat)

I said to him I was leaving, did he want to come.

MONNIE. Well, you're really confident.

IDA. He wilted over the bed, just poured on the bed, like he is now, totally apathetic. I got very turned on. I just started kissing him. He didn't do anything, y'know, move or anything. It was exciting. I kept kissing him along his neck. Then I unbuttoned his shirt and kissed him. He was acting like nothing was happening but when I opened his pants it popped straight up.

MONNIE. If you're a man, it's gonna pop up like that, like a flag pole.

IDA. There's no flag, though. There's no flag on top, so you don't have to salute. You don't have to worship them. That's the point.

MONNIE. No, but...

IDA. Love ain't a prerequisite.

MONNIE. No...a little respect, maybe.

IDA. Not even that, respect, I don't think. Not even respect, if it's what you choose.

MONNIE. I think there should be respect, a little, anyway.

IDA. Maybe. But I don't *ask* for respect. Why should I put myself in a *needy* position to *ask* for respect? If I want someone whom I don't know, whom I've seen, let's say, across the room, and there's something I want.

MONNIE. An attraction, uh-huh...

IDA. It's physical. I don't have to look for something else. It's not for breeding purposes that I have sex.

(**IDA** *covers* **TERRENCE** *with a blanket.*)

Let's just forget about him for now. He's just a body.

(*to* **TERRENCE**)

You're just a cuddle-bone, aren't you, Terrence? You're just a little cuddle-bone. Isn't that right? You're a cuddle-bone?

TERRENCE. Yeah.

MONNIE. Is he gonna be alright?

IDA. Yes, fine. He's fine.

MONNIE. I need a little snack. Do you have anything sweet? I've a sweet tooth today.

IDA. I have most of a Mars Bar left, I think. That's it. I've been eating really healthy.

(**IDA** *looks through her purse.*)

Here it is. More than three-quarters, I'd say. Go ahead.

MONNIE. Split it with me.

IDA. Ok.

MONNIE. Does he want a bite, do you think?

IDA. Do you want a bite of a Mars Bar? Terrence. Do you want a bite of a Mars Bar? God, it takes forever to get through to him. Terrence? Do you want a bite of a Mars Bar?

TERRENCE. Yes.

(**TERRENCE** *holds a hand out from under the blanket.*)

IDA. Break off a little piece.

MONNIE. Here.

(**MONNIE** *gives it to* **IDA** *who puts it in* **TERRENCE**'s *hand.*)

IDA. Here, pussy. Pussy, pussy, pussy.

(They watch as it disappears under the blanket. They chew in silence.)

MONNIE. I'm glad you called. I've been feeling...well...I don't know.

(sighs)

The world is horrible. I think I'm really unhappy in it.

(IDA. *(sympathetically)* Now...

MONNIE. Except for you, I am.

IDA. That's how I feel, too, a lot of the time I feel it's horrible.

MONNIE. I watched a bee go from flower to flower and it really hit me because I feel like I don't have a purpose, really, there's nothing.

IDA. You've got to be careful looking at nature, if you're not feeling up about things.

MONNIE. I don't pay nature any thought at all. I'm not that objective a person. I was walking by this little private garden and I was thinking, Why am I going on? It never leads anywhere, and without even planning to, you know, I stopped in thought, so lost, so upset, so alone...and I saw the bee. I got so depressed. I didn't turn back, though. I went on with my day.

IDA. That's the thing, to keep moving.

MONNIE. One of those big black bees, you know, with a purpose in life. There would be a result. There would be honey.

IDA. It doesn't do any good to get worked up about something you have no control over!

MONNIE. I need to take my mind off myself.

IDA. That's why I wanted you to come over and meet Terrence.

MONNIE. *(after a pause)* He's asleep. So peaceful.

IDA. He's playing possum.

*(**MONNIE** lifts the blanket to look at **TERRENCE**.)*

MONNIE. He looks asleep.

IDA. Maybe.

MONNIE. He's not bad looking. He's clean. One or two spots on his face could stand sanding. He's probably gonna lose some hair. Get fatter probably, if he isn't careful. Get fatter and fatter and bald with ugly skin, if he doesn't watch it.

IDA. He's mentally challenged.

>   *(beat)*
>
>   He really is. Mentally challenged. It took a while to realize.

MONNIE. No. Is he? Mentally challenged. No.

IDA. You don't notice at first, but, mentally, he's an eleven year old.

MONNIE. Stop.

IDA. Ask him. That's what he told me. At least he's aware of it. He said he was eleven. He said he was mentally challenged.

MONNIE. Oh, my God, Ida!

>   *(whispers emphatically)*
>
>   And you've been fucking him!?

IDA. All weekend.

MONNIE. No…!

>   *(beat)*
>
>   What's his name again?

IDA. Terrence.

MONNIE. Are you, Terrence, are you mentally challenged?

IDA. You have to repeat everything about ten times until he understands.

>   *(beat; to **TERRENCE**)*
>
>   Didn't you tell me you were mentally challenged? Terrence? Didn't you tell me you were mentally challenged? Terrence? Didn't you tell me you were mentally challenged?

TERRENCE. Yes.

IDA. See?

MONNIE. How old are you then? Terrence? How old are you then, if you're mentally challenged? Terrence? How old are you then, if you're mentally challenged? Terrence? How old are you?

TERRENCE. Sixteen.

IDA. He told me eleven.

(beat; to **TERRENCE***)*

You told me you were eleven. Do you remember telling me you were eleven? Terrence? Mentally? Do you remember that you told me you were mentally eleven?

TERRENCE. Yes.

IDA. See?

TERRENCE. I'm sixteen…emotionally.

IDA. Sixteen emotionally and eleven mentally? Terrence? Sixteen emotionally and eleven mentally?

(to **MONNIE***)*

This is so irritating.

MONNIE. You have to be patient.

IDA. Terrence? Is it eleven mentally and sixteen emotionally?

TERRENCE. Yes.

MONNIE. And *physically?* What age are you *physically?* Terrence? I understand you're eleven mentally and sixteen emotionally but what are you *physically?* Obviously you're much older *physically.* What's your *physical* age? What are you *physically?* May I know?

TERRENCE. Yes.

MONNIE. What is it? What age, physically?

TERRENCE. Twenty seven.

IDA. Sit up, so Monnie can look at you. Sit up, Terrence.

MONNIE. Just so I can look. I won't bite you.

IDA. Sit up, little pussy.

MONNIE. Sit up for the last little piece of Mars Bar.

IDA. Sit up, Terrence.

MONNIE. Sit up.

IDA. Sit up.

MONNIE. Pussy wants some candy?

IDA. Pussy's got to sit up. Sit, sit, sit so Monnie can take a good look. Sit the fuck up, for Christ's sake!

(**TERRENCE** *sits up.* **MONNIE** *feeds him the last bite of Mars Bar.*)

MONNIE. He could be any age almost. You could be good looking, as it goes, if you made an attempt, y'know, very presentable.
(*pause*)
I'll bet you have a nice smile.

IDA. Let her see you smile, Terrence.

MONNIE. I'll bet you have a smile in there somewhere to show me.

IDA. Let's see your smile.

MONNIE. Come on.

IDA. You showed me your loaf. So let me see you smile. Terrence, you showed me your loaf, didn't you, so let's see your smile, now.

MONNIE. God, he is a challenge.

IDA. I told you. You showed penis you can show teeth!

MONNIE. Show some teeth! Show us. You know how. Come on, show us. Smile. We're going to love it. Right? Right Ida?

IDA. Of course, we are. Smile for Monnie.

MONNIE. Smile.

IDA. Smile.

MONNIE. Smile.

IDA. Smile, fuckhead!

(**TERRENCE** *smiles.*)

(*brightly, encouraging*)
OK, then, alright.

MONNIE. That's not so bad, is it?

(*looks closer*)
They are a little stained, but it is a nice smile. One of

your nicest qualities. You want to keep a nice smile like that, go easy on candy, and brush good. At least three times.

IDA. You can stop smiling.

MONNIE. You can stop now, Terrence.

IDA. Stop smiling!

(He stops.)

MONNIE. You can remember that, Terrence? You can remember to brush three times? Terrence? Three times a day?

IDA. Answer Monnie, Terrence!

MONNIE. Let's be patient with him, Ida.

IDA. Fuck it. I'm tired of repeating myself. Can you brush three fucking times a day or not? Fucking Yes or No!

MONNIE. Maybe he already does. Is that it, Terrence. Do you? Do you brush three times? Is it already a part of your day?

TERRENCE. Yes.

MONNIE. See?

TERRENCE. I brush three times.

MONNIE. He was confused. That's all, right, Terrence? The question confused you? Isn't that it? Isn't that it, Terrence?

IDA. Were you confused? Answer, Monnie.

TERRENCE. Yes.

MONNIE. That's OK.

TERRENCE. I'm going to shower.

IDA. Go ahead. I said, OK. Go ahead.

TERRENCE. I'm going to, OK. Fuck you both.

(TERRENCE exits to shower.)

MONNIE. A little spark. "Fuck you both." A little anger, at least.

IDA. I think he likes you.

MONNIE. *(pause; quietly)* You'd never know, you know, that he's that way, not really, unless you were told. Y'know, challenged that way? I'd never actually believe it.

IDA. I know.

MONNIE. Until it's pointed out.

IDA. You could tell though, right?

MONNIE. Once you told me, yes, but I wouldn't have known.

IDA. Because he's functional and you think he has a kind of quality, at first, not just the *zero quality*,

MONNIE. You could say an easily led quality.

IDA. It's a sexy quality to me.

MONNIE. A little too passive for me.

IDA. Well…you never know…Don't knock it till ya try it.

MONNIE. Ida…!

IDA. Well – Oh, and get this. He has a twin brother.

MONNIE. What?

IDA. He has a twin.

MONNIE. No.

IDA. Yes, he does.

MONNIE. You met him?

IDA. He lives in England.

MONNIE. An identical twin?

IDA. That's what he said. Who lives in England.

MONNIE. Do you think he's that way like Terrence? You think he's mentally challenged?

IDA. How weird would that be?

MONNIE. A child in a man's body, and a twin to boot. You can pick 'em.

IDA. There's a communication, a telepathy, I guess, in twins, even over great distances, a feel for what the other is doing, because, you know, I felt someone was watching when I was mounted on him during the rain storm. It made it exciting with the rain pounding outside. I was looking down at him, really riding him, when I felt someone else was looking at me. I said to him, God, I feel like we're being watched, and I realized it felt like someone watching through him, looking through him at me. Terrence, I said, do you feel it? Can you feel we're being watched right now. Right now, Terrence, it's like someone is watching me do this to you. That's when I found out about the twin.

MONNIE. I feel we're like that at times. Monnie and Ida. Something comes over me concerning you, like being with this guy. I knew you'd met someone. So when you said come over before you go to work, I knew it was to meet someone. Some guy. Some sexy guy that turned your love light on.

IDA. We are in tune like twins, aren't we? You and I? Don't you think we're in tune like twins?

MONNIE. Yes. Psychic twins.

IDA. Stay and visit with him. I've got to go to work. Stay and visit and get acquainted. I want you to stay and, y'know, maybe you'll take an interest, and it'll work out.

(*beat*)

It's been awhile, right, since you've got laid.

MONNIE. He's not my type, though.

IDA. Well...stay and act friendly for me, try and show an interest. Try him, you never know. I'm gonna tell him I'm going. Stay for awhile. You gonna stay? Monnie, are you gonna stay for awhile. Are you? Monnie?

MONNIE. Yes.

IDA. You'll come 'round my dinner break, though, right, Monnie? You'll come 'round then, 'round seven, and you can tell me how you got along?

MONNIE. Seven?

IDA. Seven, OK?

MONNIE. Seven. OK, I'll come by.

(**IDA** *puts on a nurse's uniform and shouts to* **TERRENCE.**)

IDA. I'm going to work. I'm going to the hospital. You hear? Terrence? Monnie's gonna stay and visit. I'm going to work at the hospital and Monnie's going to keep you company for awhile. OK? Monnie's going to keep you company? I said Monnie's going to keep company while I'm at work at the hospital. OK? OK? OK? Terrence? Just fucking say yes!

TERRENCE. *(off stage)* Yes, OK, fucking yes I heard you!

IDA. *(to* **MONNIE***)* I don't have any patience. I think it's stress from seeing the little kids at work, little babies, so helpless, and with all the tubes in them. Wires. Hooked up to machines. The ones that survive, I mean, what kind of fucking life do they have? Bodies in agony.

(pause)

You're going to kiss me goodbye aren't you? Monnie? You gonna kiss me? You gonna kiss me bye-bye. Let me think about you. Come over here, kiss me and let me think about you. Monnie? Come over here, so I'll think good thoughts.

(IDA *kisses* **MONNIE** *and exits.* **TERRENCE** *is heard rapping in the shower. Moments pass.* **TERRENCE** *enters with a towel wrapped around his middle.)*

MONNIE. Do you like rap? Rap music? Well, do you? I'm asking by way of making conversation. Terrence? You know, rap, I'm asking if you like it? Do you? Terrence? Do you like rap? Rap music?

TERRENCE. Yes.

*(***TERRENCE** *sits on the bed.)*

MONNIE. They say the same thing over and over. Once is enough, if it's obvious, don't you think, Terrence? That if it's the same thing, once is enough?

(beat)

But you like it, do you? You really like rap, or are you just saying it? Terrence, do you really like rap or are you just saying?

(beat)

You want to know my opinion on the subject? I don't like it because the same thing is said over and over. But if you like it, you like it. Do you?

(beat)

Hello?

TERRENCE. I guess.

MONNIE. Even though they say the same thing over and over? Even though the same thing is said over and over, you like it, Terrence? The same thing? The identical same thing?

(pause)

Ok. I guess it's the slang you like. The latest slang, saying the same thing over and over in the latest slang. The simple minded rhymes. The simple minded forced rhymes. What else makes you like it? The beat? The same beat with little variation. The same thing said over and over in the latest slang in simple minded forced rhymes to the same beat? Is that why you like it? Terrence?

(under breath)

Maybe it's generational. Age. An age thing.

*(to **TERRENCE**)*

Do you think it's age? Terrence? Do you think it's age that makes the difference. Why you like it and I don't? Is it the age difference? We don't have to like the same thing but in this case, rap, do you think age has anything to do with it? Terrence? Is it age? Is it age, Terrence? What do you think?

(talks to herself)

I don't know what Ida sees in him. Her little pussy. Little pussy cat. I'm trying, though, trying for Ida.
Ida likes you. She'd like us to be friends. So, we should try. I'm not going to treat you like she does. That's what you might need but it's not my style. I don't like the passive type. I like the aggressive type personality in a man. The alpha mold. She likes it that you aren't an active man. She likes to be in control and dictate the action. I don't. So don't look for that in me. She likes it that you don't make a move. It turns her on. She likes it when you curl up like a pussy cat. You purr when your head's scratched. Pussy likes a head rub. You're not my type, though, I told you. You're Ida's little pussy

cat. You want your head rubbed. You want it scratched. You want to lie and be worshiped. You want it rubbed. Pussy wants to be rubbed. Pussy acts like she doesn't but she does. She wants to be scratched and rubbed. Rub rub that's for you, isn't it?! I told you, though, I like a man that knows what he wants and takes it. He's gonna hold me, y'know, he's gonna grip me in his hard hands. His personality is going to overcome me. His energy is going to electrify me. He's aggressive. Not a pussy. Not a purring pussy. Not someone waiting to be told what to do. He doesn't like the same thing over and over! He doesn't like rap, my man! He doesn't like rap music!

TERRENCE. Kent doesn't like rap.

MONNIE. Kent?

TERRENCE. I have a feeling he doesn't like rap. He used to, maybe he still does, but I've a feeling Kent doesn't now.

MONNIE. And who is Kent? Terrence? Terrence?

TERRENCE. My brother.

MONNIE. The one in England? Your twin? Ida told me you had one. Terrence? Kent is your twin brother in England?

TERRENCE. He's not there anymore. I have that feeling.

MONNIE. Where is he now? Terrence? Where is Kent now if he's not in England?

TERRENCE. Traveling. That's the feeling I get. He's not challenged like me. Kent takes charge. He knows what to do. He's popular. Outspoken. Don't worry about that, alright. Don't you worry about that part. Kent doesn't like rap. He doesn't like it, and he knows how to take over.

Scene 2

(Hospital cafe. Hospital cafe sounds. **IDA**, *in uniform, enters carrying a tray with a salad on it. She crosses toward a table, and becomes aware she's being observed.)*

IDA. Look at him sniffing the air. Shirt over his shoulder. Tattoos down his arms. Mr. Muscles. Bad as a dog ready to jump anything that moves.

(makes a more seductive body posture)

You want something, Mr. Muscles? This it? Look at him stare. Look at his eyes getting all narrow. Smells me. Smells what I have.

(loudly dismissive)

Wrong approach, fella! Helpless and lost, he might have a chance.

*(***MONNIE*** enters hurriedly.)*

MONNIE. Sorry, I'm late. Traffic's so awful.

IDA. Sit down. I'll get you something.

MONNIE. I'm not hungry.

IDA. I'll get you something sweet.

MONNIE. Maybe a little ice cream.

IDA. Cherry vanilla?

MONNIE. If they have it…of anything really.

IDA. Sit down. A little cherry vanilla coming up.

*(***IDA*** exits.* **MONNIE** *nibbles at lettuce from* **IDA**'s *plate.)*

MONNIE. Vinaigrette…All the different tastes. All the things on the tongue, in the mouth…all the things that go in. When you think about it, we're very oral as a people. All the licks, sucks, bites, the swallows…all the things soft and hard…the textures, so soft and so hard. I wonder what the twin is like? Kent. He sounds so adventurous…traveling…taking charge…a twin, but the opposite of Dough Boy…

(**MONNIE** *realizes she's being observed.*)

Oh? Look at him over there with the big strong masculine nose. Could be an alpha dog. Could come growling. Grab me by the neck in his wide mouth. Hold me down. Snarl over me.

(*shows more neck*)

See my neck? See it? Practically taste it, I'll bet.

(**IDA** *enters with ice cream.*)

IDA. A little cherry vanilla.

MONNIE. There was a man on the perimeter paying quite a bit of predatory attention to me.

IDA. They try and make a quick pick-up while the wife gets her chemo treatment.

(*They eat.*)

IDA. You had a nice visit with Terrence?

MONNIE. So-so.

IDA. Did you try?

MONNIE. What?

IDA. You know.

MONNIE. There has to be chemistry for me.

IDA. You have to create your opportunity.

MONNIE. I like a different man than you.

IDA. I know you do.

MONNIE. More grandiose than comatose.

IDA. Terrence is grandiose where it counts.

MONNIE. I'm just gonna have to wait, I guess, for my kind of guy, y'know.

IDA. When was your last time, though? Over a year.

MONNIE. There aren't any real men left. I'm a little mouse, really, a little mouse in a field, that's how I am inside, and no eagle swoops down for me. I need someone to make me forget who I am. I don't mean just anyone. I mean by a wolf or a falcon. Someone that's more than me, not less. I'm a little mouse, really, a little mouse in a field.

IDA. *(comforting her)* There'll be someone. Come on. Chin up. Don't let your ice cream melt.

(**IDA**'s *pager alarm rings.*)

This can't be good.

(reads pager's 911 code)

911. I've got to go.

MONNIE. Ok.

IDA. I'm sorry but we've got a baby in trouble might die on us.

MONNIE. Ok.

IDA. I'll see you at lunch tomorrow. OK? I'll come by court?

MONNIE. Ok. There's a specialist in a personal injury that has a bad accent and I'm going to sweat stress bullets.

IDA. Just remember you're the best stenographer there is.

MONNIE. I'm sorry it didn't click for me with Terrence.

IDA. As long as you tried…

(**IDA**'s *pager alarm rings again.*)

Oh, God. This isn't a good day.

(She exits. **MONNIE** *spoons up her cherry vanilla.)*

MONNIE. I'll just eat my ice-cream. Eat my cherry vanilla. I can be alone for ever. Waiting. Picking out the cherries while I wait for a real man. No helpless boy that needs a momma. No mamma's boy. A man. I can wait and wait and wait. So don't fucking cry for me, Argentina.

Scene 3

*(**IDA**'s studio apartment. **TERRENCE** is slurping soda through a straw in a Super-sized take-out. **IDA** is heard from the bathroom.)*

IDA. *(off)* You have to do it for me. You're gonna try real hard and concentrate. People a lot younger than you mentally do a lot more difficult things than what I'm asking. They have flown planes. They have played the violin to thousands. They have been champions of the world in chess and gymnastics. They have been computer experts. People mentally younger have saved lives. You just have to try hard and do what I tell you.

*(**TERRENCE** hits the bottom of the container to knock the last of the ice into his mouth.)*

IDA. *(off)* You can do that for me? Terrence? You can do what I'm asking? You can do that for me?

*(**IDA** enters partially clothed. Hair in rollers.)*

IDA. Did you hear me? Terrence!?

TERRENCE. Huh?

IDA. Did you hear what I've been talking about?

TERRENCE. *(shrugs)* Yeah.

IDA. What?

TERRENCE. Huh?

IDA. What have I been saying to you?

(a pause)

About Monnie? I've been talking about you and Monnie.

TERRENCE. I know, yeah.

IDA. What have I been saying?

TERRENCE. Pretend I'm the boss of her. I heard you. Say to her, "Come here. Come over here so I can look at you." I heard what you said.

IDA. Slowly with command, though.

TERRENCE. Yeah.

IDA. Look at her when you say it, and say it slower and more commanding.

TERRENCE. (*slowly*) Come here so I can look at you.

IDA. "You're mine tonight" is good too. You can make up things. It's a secret game we play on Monnie. The *boss of Monnie* game.

TERRENCE. I don't feel like a boss.

IDA. You're a boss, Terrence. You hear me? You're a boss of Monnie. That's the way to look at it.

TERRENCE. Yeah? OK. I'm the boss.

IDA. But not to me. You're not my boss. Come here. Come here, I said!

(*She rubs his crotch.*)

Monnie but not me. You are like that with Monnie. But with me you're not. Right? How are you with Monnie?

TERRENCE. Tell her what to do?

IDA. That's right. You're the boss with her. She wants you to be. You can hold her tight. You can tell her, "don't talk!"

TERRENCE. Ok.

IDA. How are you with me?

TERRENCE. Huh?

IDA. You're my little pussy cat, that's what. You can boss Monnie but you're my little pussy cat. You're her big bad dog but you're my quiet little pussy. You growl at her but you purr for me. You purr and I rub you. Rub my little pussy.

(*She stops rubbing his crotch to take the rollers out of her hair.*)

You get to make it disappear into Monnie and you get to make it disappear into me. You make it disappear like magic. Now you see it now you don't. You're a lucky little boy today, Terrence, a lucky boy. You get to be a man tonight. Lucky little boy gets to be a man with Monnie. A man with two women!

TERRENCE. Ok.

IDA. Sure, that's the spirit. It's the attitude she's looking for. You can do that. You only have to assert yourself. She's a little mouse, really. She says so herself. It's nothing you can't handle.

TERRENCE. She just needs to be taken charge of, right?

IDA. I've got to look after Monnie. She is my one true woman friend. It's a game, really. Look at it that way.

TERRENCE. *(squirms; under his breath) (English accent)*
My fucking brother.

IDA. I didn't hear you.

TERRENCE. Huh?

IDA. Speak up!

TERRENCE. I say, "come over here" and that stuff to her, right?

IDA. Yeah, to Monnie you say that, but not to me. There's a Terrence for Monnie, and then there's a Terrence for Ida. OK? OK, Terrence? Big man boss for Monnie. Little boy pussy for Ida. That's all. You'll get it. It's our little game. Big man boss for Monnie. Little boy pussy for Ida. You got it Terrence?

TERRENCE. Huh? Yeah.

IDA. Say it, Terrence. Say it with me. Big man boss for Monnie. Little boy pussy for Ida. Come on…Big man… Come on…

TERRENCE. Big man…

IDA. That's right. Big man what?

TERRENCE. Big man boss.

IDA. For who?

TERRENCE. Monnie!

IDA. Little boy pussy for Ida.

TERRENCE. Big man boss for Monnie.

IDA. Little boy pussy for Ida.

TERRENCE. *(starting to get it)* Little boy pussy for Ida.

IDA. That's good, Terrence. We'll make a good surprise for Monnie. A surprise to make Monnie happy. I'm gonna go meet her now. You stay here and remember the game we're gonna play. You stay and practice 'till I get back and you show me how well you do.

(IDA exits.)

TERRENCE. *(increasingly anxious)* Little pussy for Ida. Big man for Monnie. Little pussy. Big man. Pussy for Ida. Man for Monnie. Little. Big. Little. Big.

Scene 4

(The courthouse patio. **MONNIE** *and* **IDA** *eat with chopsticks from take out containers.)*

IDA. He has a whole other side to him.

MONNIE. That'd surprise me.

IDA. I was impressed to see it.

MONNIE. Coming out of his cocoon, huh?

IDA. This manly thing, y'know?

MONNIE. I'd have to see it to believe it.

IDA. Maybe he's feeling more at home. He takes charge more.

MONNIE. It's hard to picture.

IDA. It's nothing I want, a personality change in that direction, that's for sure.

(eats)

The chicken and cashew is good.

MONNIE. It's alright, yeah.

IDA. I'm glad you're over the hump on this witness you had.

MONNIE. Thank God. He's an expert on the cause of death and I could hardly understand him. You can't let that show too much, y'know, that you're having trouble. There are a hundred court recorders just waiting to get a foot in the door.

(They eat.)

IDA. The guy was foreign, the specialist?

MONNIE. *(food in mouth)* Boston. Terrible accent.

IDA. *(food in mouth)* Same thing.

MONNIE. What?

IDA. *(gestures, swallows; then clearer)* The same. Fucking Boston. Foreign.

MONNIE. Yeah, he couldn't speak English right.

IDA. Come by for a drink. Celebrate your victory over circumstance.

MONNIE. I don't know. He's going to be there?

IDA. See if you see what I mean. Maybe I imagined it. My worse fear, y'know, a boss in bed with me.

MONNIE. I don't know.

(eats)

This is good. This is spicy.

Did that baby die? The one yesterday?

IDA. You can't get attached, you know, you'd go crazy.

MONNIE. It'd get to me.

IDA. It gets to me too, Monnie, but what are you going to do?

MONNIE. I'm sorry.

IDA. Yeah. Well...

(pause)

I got that good vodka.

MONNIE. The Polish vodka?

IDA. The Polish buffalo grass vodka.

MONNIE. I'm tempted. You've got me tempted now.

IDA. We can party, and you'll see if I'm imagining things or not. I'll get some chips and dip.

MONNIE. Ok. I guess. You think you need my opinion...

Scene 5

(IDA*'s apartment. Big band swing plays.* TERRENCE *nervously drums a hand to the music.* IDA *enters with a couple drinks.*)

IDA. You like the music? It's full of life I think. Do you like it? The music? Big band music? It's sophisticated music. Do you like it? It's swing.

TERRENCE. Yeah.

IDA. This is a vodka tonic. It'll help your confidence. Go on. It builds confidence.

(*loudly*)

It builds confidence!

(*She turns the music down.*)

Try it, you'll like it. Terrence? Try it, you'll like it. You like it? Maybe you're not used to it?

TERRENCE. It's Ok.

IDA. It's an acquired taste. You like it, though? It's vodka and tonic. Polish vodka. Good vodka.

TERRENCE. It's alright, yeah.

IDA. I usually drink it by itself. Ice cold or maybe over ice. You keep good vodka in the freezer compartment. It's an acquired taste. You know what that means, Terrence? Terrence, do you know? An acquired taste? It means you grow used to it and eventually you acquire a taste for it. You'll like it. An acquired taste. Monnie should be here soon. Drink up. It'll give you confidence.

TERRENCE. I'm OK.

IDA. It'll give you confidence!

TERRENCE. Alright.

IDA. Sit down and take it easy until she gets here. Sit down, Terrence. Sit down and take it easy. Concentrate on what I've taught you. You want to please me, don't you, Terrence? You want to please me? Right? Please the teacher?

TERRENCE. I'm the boss. I remember.

IDA. You're the boss for Monnie. Sit down. I'll be right back.

(**IDA** *exits to the kitchen.* **TERRENCE** *turns the music back up. He beats out the rhythm, as though playing a miniature drum set.* **IDA** *returns with the chips and dip. She does a simple swing step.*)

IDA. Maybe I can show you how to dance? Would you like that sometime, Terrence, to learn to dance? Dance swing?

(*loudly*)

Would you sometime like to learn how to dance swing?!

(*She turns the music down.*)

IDA. I asked if you'd like that sometime, to learn how to dance, learn how to dance swing. I could show you. Maybe you could learn. Would you like to? It's called swing. Would you? Terrence? Learn how to dance?

TERRENCE. I can dance.

IDA. No.

TERRENCE. What?

IDA. You can dance?

TERRENCE. Well…

IDA. This is a good one.

TERRENCE. Well…

IDA. You can swing?

TERRENCE. Maybe…

IDA. Swing?

TERRENCE. I think so.

IDA. You're funny.

TERRENCE. Yeah.

IDA. OK. Let's see. Let's dance.

TERRENCE. OK.

(*She turns up the music.*)

IDA. Do you lead? Do you know how to lead?

(*loudly*)

Dance then, if you dance, let's dance then.

TERRENCE. Want to dance?

IDA. What?

TERRENCE. Want to dance?

IDA. That's what I said!

TERRENCE. Ok.

(*He leads her in a swing dance for a few moves. She stops suddenly.*)

IDA. Who taught you?

TERRENCE. What?

(*She turns down the music.*)

IDA. Who taught you? Who taught you how to dance, to swing dance? Someone taught you, right? Who was it?

TERRENCE. A woman.

IDA. Who?

TERRENCE. A woman.

IDA. Did she teach how to follow, too? When I dance with Monnie, she follows. Did the woman teach you how to follow?

TERRENCE. To follow?

IDA. See if you can follow.

TERRENCE. Follow?

IDA. See if you can. Monnie does. See if you can.

(*She turns up the music. She leads, sees that he can follow. She stops. She turns off the music.*)

IDA. What woman taught you to follow? You hear me? What woman was it that taught you to follow?

TERRENCE. A woman I met once. I don't remember. Someone. My mother taught me too. She taught me to dance.

IDA. Was the woman your mother? Terrence, the woman, was it your mother? Concentrate. The woman who taught you to dance? Was that your mother? Was the woman and your mother the same? Can you answer me? Your mother was a woman wasn't she?

TERRENCE. *(confused)* Yes!

IDA. Was she the woman that taught you?

TERRENCE. She wasn't my mother, the woman, but my mother taught me, too.

(The intercom buzzes. She goes to it.)

IDA. Hello?

MONNIE. *(off) (filtered over intercom)* It's me.

IDA. Come on up.

(to **TERRENCE***)*

It's Monnie. I'm going to mix her drink. Have her drink ready and waiting. We're gonna celebrate. You're gonna be a big surprise, right? Right, Terrence? You're gonna surprise Monnie how you can be a whole other person. The kind of boss man she likes. Big boss man for Monnie!

(She exits to the kitchen. **TERRENCE** *turns up the music.* **MONNIE** *enters.)*

TERRENCE. Swing. Big band.

MONNIE. This is music I like.

TERRENCE. Me too.

IDA. *(off)* Here I come.

TERRENCE. Big band swing.

MONNIE. It's sophisticated music.

*(***IDA** *enters with* **MONNIE***'s drink.)*

IDA. Here you go.

MONNIE. Thank you.

IDA. Nothing too good for you, Monnie. Right, Terrence, nothing too good for Monnie? She's a survivor. All she puts up with at work. There's nothing too good for Monnie is there, Terrence?

TERRENCE. Right.

IDA. She has to write down everything people say in court. She's a court recorder, a stenographer. All the horrible things she has to hear day after day.

MONNIE. You're job isn't easy, though, either, is it? All the sick and dying? All the babies you care for. Helpless little things all damaged.

IDA. Well, to us then. The survivors.

(They sip their drinks.)

TERRENCE. You're looking good.

IDA. Listen to him?

MONNIE. What?

TERRENCE. You're looking good.

IDA. You're changing your spots are you?

TERRENCE. *(to MONNIE)* I could grab hold. Take charge. I can swing.

MONNIE. Listen to the big bad wolf. I'd better run to the little girls room and make sure my lipstick is still on my face.

(MONNIE exits into the bathroom.)

TERRENCE. *(brusquely)* Toss me some chips.

IDA. What?

TERRENCE. Chips.

IDA. Please.

TERRENCE. What?

IDA. You want some chips?

TERRENCE. Yeah.

IDA. Then it's *please*! Don't talk to me like I'm Monnie!

TERRENCE. I should go!

IDA. You don't have to go, but don't talk to me like I'm Monnie! You're not boss man with me! You're boss man with Monnie! You don't have to go. You have to take charge of Monnie. I take charge of you and you take charge of Monnie. Remember how when you're with me you don't do anything? Remember how I do everything? You lie down and I do everything!

(TERRENCE lies down.)

Don't lie down now. Get up now because now you're in charge of Monnie. You're the boss. Get up!

(He sits up. IDA crosses to him with the chips.)

Say please and open. Say please.

TERRENCE. Please.

(She feeds him a chip. MONNIE enters.)

MONNIE. This is music worth our time, isn't it? Is it Ok if I turn it up a little? Ok with you, Terrence, if I turn it up?

TERRENCE. Yeah.

IDA. We were just dancing before you came over, weren't we Terrence? Weren't we swing dancing before Monnie came over?

MONNIE. You and him?

IDA. Uh-huh. Dancing swing. You're gonna have to show her, Terrence. You're gonna have to give her the honor of a dance.

MONNIE. Let's wet our whistles a bit first. Get a glow.

(sips her drink)

This music is complex that's why I like it. It seems simple but it's not. There's a lot of variety. It's syncopated rhythm. Sophisticated. This good vodka helps.

TERRENCE. Polish.

MONNIE. I like good Polish vodka.

IDA. Prosit.

MONNIE. Prosit.

IDA. That's what we say to toast. It's Polish.

MONNIE. Prosit. Terrence.

TERRENCE. Prosit.

(He drinks.)

Come over here. Don't talk.

MONNIE. Well, if you insist.

IDA. I feel a little glow, that's for sure.

TERRENCE. Let's swing.

   (**IDA** *turns the music up.* **TERRENCE** *dances with* **MONNIE**. *Ida watches, then cuts in.*)

IDA. Now you follow.

   (*They dance.*)

MONNIE. Now you lead.

   (**TERRENCE** *leads* **MONNIE**.)

IDA. Now you follow.

MONNIE. Now you lead.

IDA. Now you follow.

MONNIE. Now you lead.

IDA. Follow.

MONNIE. Lead.

   (*She spins him to* **IDA**.)

IDA. Yes.

   (*She spins him to* **MONNIE**.)

MONNIE. Yes.

   (**TERRENCE** *shows signs of panic and makes to flee, but gets grabbed up in the dance.*)

MONNIE/IDA. Yes. Yes. Yes. Go. Go. We love swing. We love swing. Swing, swing, swing – let's swing!

   (**IDA** *and* **MONNIE** *dance together.* **TERRENCE** *finishes his drink, downs the remains of* **MONNIE** *and* **IDA**'s, *picks up the bottle, drinks, and passes out backwards on the bed.*)

   (**IDA** *and* **MONNIE** *dance more and more flirtatiously.*)

Scene 6

(**IDA**'s *apartment. The morning after.* **MONNIE** *is passed out in bed. Buzzer rings. She stirs. Buzzer rings.* **MONNIE** *wakes, disoriented.*)

MONNIE. *(calls thickly)* Ida?

(*Buzzer.*)

Ida?

(*Buzzer.*)

Jesus.

(*She drags herself to the intercom.*)

Yeah, hello.

(*Lights up on the downstairs exterior front entrance. A man in a black motorcycle jacket talks into the intercom box.*)

KENT. *(English accent)* I'm looking for Terrence.

MONNIE. Who?

KENT. Terrence.

MONNIE. Terrence?

KENT. I'm his brother. Kent. I'm looking for him.

MONNIE. He isn't here.

KENT. Is this Ida?

MONNIE. No. She's at work.

KENT. Do you know where I can find him then?

MONNIE. No.

KENT. He told me he had two friends, Ida and Monnie. I'm guessing Monnie? Hello?

MONNIE. What?

KENT. You're Monnie, then?

MONNIE. Yeah.

KENT. Cheers, Monnie. Nice to meet you. Terrence told me about you. Said we might get along. I've an idea. Why don't I pop up and say hello? How would that be, Monnie? If I popped up and said hello? Maybe a quick cup of tea? How's that sound, Monnie? I pop up and we have a quick cup of tea? We say hello and get acquainted? Have a laugh? What do you say?

MONNIE. I'm not dressed.

KENT. Take a minute, then. Get into something comfy. Don't get fussy for me. Toss on what's handy and buzz me up.

MONNIE. I don't think I should.

KENT. What's that? You say something?

MONNIE. You're his brother from England?

KENT. His spitting image. A dead ringer. The very same except the personality is at odds. You can already tell the difference in that department, can't you? You've gotta be tempted to see what this gob is like that won't go away. I think you are, aren't you, tempted by curiosity? You are tempted by curiosity to get a look, I'll bet, aren't you, and meet the twin brother of your friend?

MONNIE. Yes.

KENT. There. You said it yourself. Give the door a buzz. You said it yourself. You won't regret it. Go ahead. What's life without a gamble?

(She reaches out to the front door buzzer. Hesitates.)

Go on. We'll share a word about the joys of life.

MONNIE. I don't know.

KENT. Sure you do. Have a word with someone that knows up from down. You won't get a bad direction from me. I've traveled. I'm a traveler. I think Terrence might have mentioned that, if he mentioned me at all. A man of the world. Seen most things once, did them twice. Let's just say I'm a bloke that knows what he wants.

(She presses the buzzer.)

Scene 7

(A short time later. **MONNIE** *and* **KENT** *having tea.)*

KENT. A bit slow, eh? Terrence is, right? Not as quick as you'd like?

MONNIE. Well…

KENT. Ida's at work?

MONNIE. The hospital.

KENT. Works with infants, doesn't she? Sounds like someone nurturing. A nurturing instinct. That's nice to see in a person. I'll bet she found Terrence a nutter, though, right? I don't blame her. But he's my twin brother, though, and I love him as is. I could do with more tea. Fetch another cup will you, darling?

(MONNIE goes to the kitchen with his cup.)

You're a nice sized woman. Did Terrence mention we have a telepathy? He knows I'm mad for the ample proportioned esthetic in the female form. You know what I think? You're alright. Make a deadman come, as the English saying goes.

(She returns with a fresh cup of tea.)

Brilliant, thanks.

(sizes her up)

Let's have a look at you. Definitely not a poster girl for the holocaust, are you? You have size. Something to appreciate. I don't mean to embarrass you. I'm flesh myself, if you've noticed? Got myself a gut, don't I? I like to carry a stone or two over the limit. Have more to please with, don't we?

(holds his gut)

Midnight this turns to cock. But you're no elephant. You're no bloody mad cow. You're no pregnant hippo! More of a Reubens, I'd say. More of a Titian. More Wagnerian. More a beauty from the world of art at a time when women were voluptuous, manly even.

Hap'ly though, not you, luv. Not manly at all. Come on take a turn round for me. Don't be shy. That's it. Very nice. Sit down.

(**MONNIE** *sits.*)

Let's talk. What's on your mind, Monnie?

MONNIE. How long have you been in the U.S?

KENT. Not long, luv.

MONNIE. You like it…so far?

KENT. Very nice, luv, yes, thanks.

MONNIE. How about New York?

KENT. Very impressed. It's got snap. Have you traveled much?

MONNIE. I plan to.

KENT. I have traveled the world. You can be proud of your city. It compares well to Calcutta in cleanliness.

(*beat*)

Terrence was here all night, was he?

MONNIE. I think. My memory is blurry.

KENT. Had a few, did you?

MONNIE. We did, yes.

KENT. He's become quite a wag, has he?

MONNIE. We had drinks and danced the swing.

KENT. You and your girlfriend didn't take advantage of the dented sod, did you?

MONNIE. No.

KENT. A man that thinks he's eleven?

MONNIE. No.

KENT. I'm only having a wank. Do him nothing but good, if Ida's half the wonder you are.

(*He takes out a hash pipe.*)

Like a bit of this? Black hashish? From Afghanistan. Very hard to get now. Very rare.

MONNIE. No, thank you.

KENT. Don't mind me then, if I have a sample myself. You're no victim of the bourgeois double standard, are you?

MONNIE. No.

KENT. I can see you're a bit of the rebel yourself.

(lights up)

Help you out of feeling some of the dog, if you do. It's medicinal. Promotes a general feeling of well being. Asian medicine. It's herbal. I don't overdo it. I'd take a drink, but it's a little early.

(luxuriant exhale)

Ah, very comforting!

MONNIE. Well, I guess I could use some well being.

KENT. Why not? You've never tried it?

MONNIE. Well, I wouldn't say that...

(She takes a drag.)

Smooth. Thanks. I used to smoke marijuana.

KENT. The same general family of temptation.

MONNIE. I did most things when I was younger. Maybe a little more won't hurt me.

(She takes another drag – a deep one.)

KENT. How's that? Feeling a bit more comforted?

MONNIE. I think the beginnings of comfort.

KENT. Terrence told me he stayed here on the odd night of late. This is where I might find him, if he wasn't at his flat. The world's a magical place isn't it? Because without that little bit of information, and as you know, Terrence doesn't say that much as a rule, but without that I wouldn't be here.

MONNIE. I should have gone home myself but I had one too many at our little party. We all did. Your brother passed out.

KENT. He's not used to drink. He didn't become difficult, did he?

MONNIE. A little more outgoing. He is usually quite passive, isn't he?

KENT. He's always been very shy, actually.

MONNIE. One moment he was shy, let's say, and the next he was twirling me around the room. Usually he just stays curled up like a kitty. That's what Ida calls him. Her little pussy. She likes a passive man. I'm the opposite of that. I like someone with a presence. More of an alpha dog or an alpha wolf. That's how Ida and I are different. We're alike in many ways, almost twins ourselves, but the opposite of you and Terrence. You look alike but are different people inside. Ida and I don't look exactly alike, we're similar looking, in a way, we're not twins physically, but we think alike in nearly every way, except she likes a man that wants to be told what to do, a more comatose personality, that can practically play dead, actually. Well, I wonder what's got me talking all of a sudden? Anyway, I like a man that makes the decisions so I don't have to. A sense of danger about him. Grandiose. Terrence is more a pussy cat all curled up waiting to be rubbed.

KENT. That's not me, is it?

MONNIE. No, you're more a panther or a lion pacing around making decisions, traveling around the world, bringing herbal medicine back from war-torn countries.

KENT. So it wasn't an orgy you had here last night then?

MONNIE. No, but I think Terrence got scared it was turning into one. I think he may have had too much to drink and started getting ideas that were very far from the truth.

KENT. He's very impressionable.

MONNIE. He either passed out, or ran out, but I can't remember which one. The later part of the evening is all fogged up.

KENT. I've got an idea, Monnie. Let's step out and have some breakfast?

MONNIE. I could use something all right. My appetite is back all of a sudden and I wonder why? I'm gonna freshen up, though, is that OK with you?

KENT. Don't take all day.

MONNIE. Can I take a quick shower?

KENT. I might have to come in and hurry you up if you take all day.

MONNIE. Ok. I'll only be a minute. Start counting.

(She exits to the bathroom. Sound of water. He walks to the open bathroom door and looks in.)

KENT. When I was in Rome, I had melon. I bought a whole melon in the market. Big round melon. Pink. Juicy. Sweet. You hear what I'm saying? Monnie? You hear the thing about the melon? The Italian melon?

MONNIE. *(off)* I like that story. I like to hear about men's travels.

KENT. You look sweet like a melon, Monnie.

MONNIE. *(off)* Have I been in here a long time. Kent? Have I been in here too long already?

KENT. I think I might have to come in.

MONNIE. *(off)* I'm sorry. For taking too long.

KENT. I'm gonna have to come in and see what it is. I might have to do that. You hear me, Monnie? You hear what I'm saying about coming in because you're taking so long? You hear I'm coming in?

MONNIE. *(off)* Ok. If you think you have to. If that's a decision you have to make.

KENT. I think it is. I think so. I think it's one I have to make. 'Cause look at you, round like an Italian melon, naked, water running off her.

MONNIE. *(off)* Ok. Ok, then.

(He goes into the bathroom.)

KENT. *(off)* I'm inside. I'm inside now.

MONNIE. *(off)* Is that you!

KENT. *(off)* I'll get wet for you! You see that I'll get wet to claim you?!

MONNIE. *(off) (laughter)* Oh! Oh! Oh!

(Swing music up. Lights fade out.)

Scene 8

(MONNIE's studio apartment. The mirror image of IDA's. IDA and MONNIE are eating ice-cream, sharing the container.)

MONNIE. He doesn't want to see his brother, you think?

IDA. That's my opinion.

MONNIE. It's so weird, because with twins, y'know, they're so close. Then, remember the sisters were twins, one tried to kill the other?

IDA. I remember, Chinese twins, one was jealous of the other and things went bad.

MONNIE. Things might get twisted more with twins.

IDA. It's not only twins. Friends have done the same. Gotten twisted over something.

MONNIE. It's stranger if it's twins because we're looking at them, you know, seeing them as the identical same thing, but it's not the same identical thing to them, is it?

IDA. No. Because they can look exactly the same, a cell divided, the same egg divided, and have a different opinion of one another.

MONNIE. Kent said they haven't seen each since they went to Disneyworld for their eleventh birthday.

IDA. I told him his brother was in town, Kent was here, looking for him, and he put his head under the pillow. He's scared to see him, I think.

MONNIE. Where do you think he went?

IDA. The movies. He goes everyday, twice a day sometimes, I think. He just disappeared when I told him Kent showed up.

MONNIE. He knows Kent and I are friendly?

IDA. He sensed it, so I told him you were.

MONNIE. There was a moment when Kent took me in the bathroom, practically by force. I was holding on to the sink and he was behind me, really ramming away, and

I looked at him in the mirror. For a moment, when I looked, I thought of Terrence. Kent's more, I don't know, has more dash, that's for sure, and that effects the looks, the perception, but for that moment in the mirror, I thought my God it looks like I'm being fucked by Terrence, but then the growls he made… no way…the animals sounds…no way…and still in his leather jacket like an animal skin…like a wild animal had me trapped…there was no mistaking who it was. Nice to have someone pick up the check, too, without making a thing about it, y'know, it's refreshing. He did that with the breakfast check. Not a word.

IDA. I pay my own way.

MONNIE. I've treated you.

IDA. I don't let a man pay for me.

MONNIE. I don't see the difference.

IDA. I do.

MONNIE. OK.

IDA. I'll never understand how you can appreciate being raped.

MONNIE. Well, it's not rape actually.

IDA. If there's any rape being done I want to be the one doing it.

MONNIE. It's being taken. It's manly power entering you.

IDA. Forcibly, you said.

MONNIE. With force. It's fantasy, you know that.

IDA. I know it's fantasy!

MONNIE. *(brief pause)* I don't know what's keeping Kent. I'll have to go to work soon. You could stay and visit when I go. I'd like that.

IDA. No thanks.

MONNIE. You could do it for me. I'd really like you and Kent to get acquainted.

(slight English inflection)

I did for Terrence, didn't I?

IDA. You're saying things with an English accent now.

MONNIE. I am not.

IDA. I can hear it.

MONNIE. What?

IDA. Little inflections.

MONNIE. It's not true.

IDA. You get consumed and you're talking like him.

MONNIE. Well, if it is, I like being influenced. That's how I learn. He has such good speech, y'know, the pronunciation. He's English. They're definitely, I don't know, better at it. It's impressive. It's something I respect, you know, pronunciation, because I listen to it so much at work. It's what I do.

IDA. You've eaten all the pecans again, that's why I don't get chocolate pecan, because you go right for the pecans.

MONNIE. I thought you didn't like the pecans that much. I thought you got chocolate pecan because you know I like them. That's why I thought you got it.

IDA. It is, but I like to have an option. Here's one, thanks.

MONNIE. See? I look out for you.

(Intercom buzzes.)

Well…better be him.

(into intercom)

Hello. Oh, you are, are you? Last door the end of the hall.

(to IDA)

Let him in. I'll just freshen myself up.

(She takes up the ice cream carton.)

I think we're through with you.

*(**MONNIE** exits. A knock at the door. **KENT** enters with two bottles of wine.)*

KENT. Ta. You must be Ida.

MONNIE. *(off)* I'll be right out. Say hello to Ida.

KENT. *(calls off to* **MONNIE***)* I'm doing that, luv, don't rush yourself.

(to **IDA***)*

Bet you can't guess who I am?

MONNIE. *(off)* I've got to go to work you know.

KENT. Terrence is a lucky sod to have you caring about him, I'd say. I went around to your flat hoping to surprise him. He's not with you?

IDA. No.

KENT. You're not keeping him locked in a room so I can't see him are you?

*(***MONNIE** *enters. He holds up the bottles.)*

Libations.

MONNIE. I have to leave in seconds.

KENT. I would have been here sooner but the bank took forever. I'm looking at some property, you see, beach property. Then I was running back and forth trying to find Terrence. I half think he's avoiding me. Fetch us a cork screw, like a good girl.

MONNIE. You know I have to work.

KENT. You've time for a toast. A small one won't hurt, will it? Ease the pain of being away from me.

MONNIE. *(to* **IDA***)* Isn't he cheeky?

(to **KENT***)*

I can't go in smelling of alcohol.

(She exits to the kitchen.)

KENT. *(calls out to* **MONNIE***)* That's why I've brought some breath mints, isn't it? Glasses too, luv.

(to **IDA***)*

Knows how to please a man, Monnie does. Good sense of humor, too.

(calls out to **MONNIE***)*

I've leased the car I told you I wanted, the Malibu

convertible. Red with a white top. Only kind to have in summer, isn't it? You can show me the sights. We'll take a spin out to the Island.

(to **IDA***)*

What do you drive? You do drive, don't you Ida?

IDA. No.

KENT. What would it be if you did? You'd have something lively to sport around in, I'll bet? A girl of your dash, right? Conceptually. What would be the automobile of your choice? What car would make you feel like a master of the road? Something sharp, I'll bet? Something wisely chosen, I'm sure, so if you drove, Ida, what would it be?

IDA. I don't know…Hundai, Elantra?

(He has a big laugh.)

KENT. Sensible, reliable motoring, is it then?

*(***MONNIE** *returns with glasses and a corkscrew.)*

MONNIE. I've never been to the Hamptons.

KENT. We can all go. Tour the area. I wouldn't mind running into Billy Joel. Stop off and say hello, you think? Do some harmony with the Piano Man. I'm not interested in any of the anorectic movie stars that flock there summers with their huge breasts given 'em by the doctor, though. No point with two healthy ladies in the car. What do you say? Beaujolais or Zinfandel? Zinfandel I think for now. Let's save the Beaujolais for after dark.

(He starts opening the wine.)

I was hoping Terrence would be here. I think he gets shy around me, embarrassed. My success, you see? He doesn't mind spending my money, though. I don't mind either as long as he isn't taken advantage of. He's not is he? You wouldn't say that of him, would you? Ida? You wouldn't say Terrence is being taken advantage of by anyone that you know of, would you? He's not is he? Because, as you know, he is a bit south in a northerly facing room, so to speak.

(He pops the cork.)

Ah, here we are. Let's pour. Not a bad color. Bright rich pink rosé. Nice hint of tartness with a subtle lemony bouquet. Ah, yes, a dry fruity woody slightly nutty bite and a dark soothing earthy summery after taste tinged with regret. I think you're going to enjoy this. Paso Robles, 1998, remember the year ladies. How about your thoughts, now, Ida? Terrence isn't being used by anyone? Led astray in harmful ways, is he? You're looking after him, right? Making sure he's not led up the garden path? You'd know it, right, wouldn't you? You'd know if Terrence was being led astray in harmful ways, wouldn't you?

MONNIE. Of course she'd know, wouldn't you? You'd know if he were, wouldn't you? Ida? Wouldn't you know if Terrence was being led astray in harmful ways?

KENT. You can answer here among friends.

IDA. I don't see him all the time.

MONNIE. But it isn't anything you've heard is it? He's not mentioned anything has he? There've been no hints have there? That's all Kent wants to know. Out of concern for his brother, right?

(to **KENT***)*

That's all?

KENT. Tell us if you've heard anything, that's all, like your friend Monnie says. Have you?

MONNIE. You can answer, can't you, Ida? Be polite.

KENT. Terrence's state of antefunctionalism isn't catching, is it?

IDA. No.

MONNIE. She's kind of in shock from seeing you. It's like seeing him. I felt the same way at first. Is that it? Is that it, Ida? The identical thing is a bit confusing, isn't it? The fact they look alike and act differently? Is that what it is?

IDA. Maybe.

MONNIE. You're used to Terrence being more of a non verbal type of person and to see how he is if he's not confuses you.

KENT. I've a little of him in me when I'm quiet. Either I've nothing to say or I don't shut up. Talking comes of knowing what you're talking about, though, doesn't it? And that's not exactly his forte, so to speak. Let's toast Terrence then, even though he's not here. A toast in absentia. To Terrence, and our reunion. In the very near future, I hope.

(They drink.)

KENT. Mmmm, yes, there's a grape that sends a message to the French.

MONNIE. I've gotta go. I hate to.

KENT. Don't forget the breath freshener I brought.

MONNIE. It's good to have some English manners about the place. It's good to be around a cultured person.

KENT. My pleasure.

MONNIE. I can use the influence. Maybe I'd learn to appreciate things more.

KENT. You've time to finish your glass. Just let me pop into the W.C. a minute. Give it a drain.

MONNIE. Through there, the first door.

*(**KENT** exits to the bathroom.)*

*(to **IDA**)*

I've got to go to the court house. Stay and visit, get acquainted.

IDA. He's not my type of personality, the shit head type personality.

MONNIE. Well…be friendly for me, try and show an interest. Do it for me. You never know. I'm gonna tell him I'm going. Stay for a while. You never know, you might get along. Try, at least. I tried with Terrence. You gonna stay? Ida, are you gonna stay for a while? If you are I'm gonna tell him. Are you? Are you going to stay? Ida? You'll stay and get acquainted won't you Ida?

IDA. Yes.

MONNIE. You'll come round my break, though, right Ida? You'll come round then? Tell me how you got along? You'll come round? Say four?

IDA. Four?

MONNIE. Or four-thirty, let's say. OK?

IDA. OK, I'll come by.

(**MONNIE** *moves to talk into the bathroom.*)

MONNIE. I'm going to work. I'm going to court. I'm going to work, you hear, Kent? Ida's gonna stay and visit. I'm going to work and Ida's going to keep you company for a while. Ok? Ida's going to keep you company? I said Ida's going to keep company while I'm at work. Ok? Ok? Ok? Kent?

KENT (*off stage*) Yes, Ok, fucking yes, I heard you. Let me finish my piss will you?

MONNIE. (*to* **IDA**) You're going to kiss me goodbye aren't you?

IDA. Come over here, then.

MONNIE. Kiss me and let me think about you. Ida? I'll think good thoughts.

(*They kiss.* **KENT** *enters.*)

KENT. Some of my best friends are lesbians.

MONNIE. Don't be cheeky.

KENT. I appreciate the closeness between my women friends.

MONNIE. We're not lesbians, though, are we Ida?

(*to* **KENT**)

You should know better, shouldn't you?

(**KENT** *puts his arms around* **MONNIE**.)

KENT. Nothing you like better than a real man in you. Nothing Monnie likes more than a caveman taking charge, don't you agree, Ida? I've found her secret, don't you think? Provided there's a stiff willy in service.

MONNIE. You're terrible. He's terrible, isn't he, Ida? She knows I like a man with authority. Don't mess up my dress. I can't turn my back or he's humping my leg. You'll make me late. Come on, now, you've got to let me go. Doesn't he? Ida? Tell him he's got to let me go.

KENT. I could make you stay, couldn't I?

MONNIE. You won't though, will you?

KENT. I guess you can go. I'll make it up to you when you get off tonight.

MONNIE. Ida's gonna stay and keep company, so you can get acquainted.

KENT. We're practically related already.

MONNIE. OK, then, and you'll make it up to me later. I heard you.

KENT. We'll have some fun. Come here and give us a kiss.

(She moves closer to him and he backs away.)

Come on, come here, and kiss us goodbye.

(She moves closer and he backs away.)

Come here now.

*(**MONNIE** moves to **KENT**. He grabs her tightly and runs his hands over her.)*

MONNIE. Bye then. Don't do anything I wouldn't.

*(**MONNIE** exits.)*

KENT. This is good. It's good to have this time alone with you. Alone with Terrence's new friend Ida. Sort things out.

IDA. Just don't try to shove your balls down my throat.

KENT. Have a set of your own, do you?

IDA. I've a collection.

KENT. Brings us to Terrence, doesn't it? I always thought he was a bit of a ponce.

IDA. A what?

KENT. A bit of a fag. That's why he runs when he sees me coming. Thinks I won't approve. He'll get over it.

We're very close. As close you can get. It's the same with you and your girlfriend, isn't it? The feeling of what's happening to the other? Like when I was having my way with Monnie. I thought what's this sensation come over me? It stopped me dead in my tracks. I could almost see you and him. Took me by surprise. But you wouldn't be bent over the furnishings, would ya, luv? You want the man on the bottom. Like him helpless. Like to take prisoners. Terrence is a baby. He lets you play the man. He's no challenge, really, is he? That's why I say he's a bit of a ponce. Still, he has to be engorged, doesn't he? Something of a corpse with a mast at full sail. Comatose with a hard one for you to have fun with. Women are capable of more variety than men. More sensual pleasure in more forms. That's a well known fact. Though they rightly feel more natural when men take charge and dominate them sexually, and, in the end, after the warfare, that is the role nature gave us. We're not insects are we? Women eat the men there, but we're higher mammals. We've large brains. You want someone that's gonna take charge you can trust, don't you, Ida? Someone shows you he's capable of taking care of you. There's a fear you have, isn't there, a fear of letting go of yourself. You think you've struck it rich with Terrence. A man that thinks he's eleven. Eleven in a body like mine. I'm not eleven, Ida.

IDA. And I'm not Monnie, so don't beat your fucking chest to impress me!

KENT. You'd like to be taken for a change, wouldn't you? You'd like to leave Terrence locked up with his little bowl of milk and roll around and fuck in the jungle like a real woman. You want to go to animal land, don't you? You want to wander into the meadow where the bull is waiting. Your hips are for mounting. You have flesh. You have size. You want to be ridden until you break, until you ache, until you offer yourself up like a sacrifice on a stake. What you really want is to submit, isn't it?

IDA. You touch me and I'll put your head through the floor.

KENT. Listen to you.

IDA. You heard dickbrain.

KENT. I respect you because you're Monnie's good friend but I know what a bloody cow you can be, don't I?

IDA. What did you call me?

KENT. A bloody fucking cow fucking bloody cunt that takes advantage of a mentally challenged man.

(She gets him around the neck in a head lock.)

IDA. I'm a bloody fucking cow fucking bloody cunt, am I?

KENT. I won't do violence with a woman.

IDA. Is this violence?

(She rams his head into the wall.)

KENT. Yes. Stop it.

IDA. You want to take back you called me a bloody fucking cunt?

KENT. No.

IDA. Take it back.

(Rams his head.)

KENT. Ok.

IDA. Ok, what?

KENT. I take it back.

IDA. You've something else insulting to say?

KENT. Nothing.

IDA. You're sure, nothing?

KENT. Nothing.

(She throws him to the floor.)

IDA. Talk to me like that again, I'll put you in the hospital. You hear me? You hear if you talk to me like that again I'll put you in the hospital? You hear what I said will happen?

(She grabs him by the head.)

KENT. Let me go. I don't want to be violent. Let me go.

IDA. I can make you roll over and bark if I want.

KENT. I can't breathe.

IDA. You know I could, don't you? Don't you?

KENT. Yes.

IDA. I can make you roll over and piss in the air. 'Cause under the big bully is a little fairy faggot man.

(She lets him go.)

Sit down. Sit down.

(He sits.)

KENT. I want to see Terrence.

IDA. We have an understanding now? We have gotten acquainted, haven't we? You know I'm not Monnie, right? Kent? You know I'm not Monnie?

KENT. Yes.

IDA. You understand we're different, now, so I'm glad we talked. You hear? I'm glad we understand each other.

KENT. I want to see Terrence.

IDA. We'll all get together. Now that there is an understanding. Now that you know we're not all the same thing. Now that you know there are these differences.

*(**IDA** exits.)*

KENT. Fucking cow. Fucking bloody fucking cow. Fucking cow cunt. Fucking bloody fucking cow cunt. Terrence, you rotten sod, rotten sod pussy! Terrence, you pissy retarded sissy fucking bloody fucking cow!

(screaming)

YOU WEAK FUCK. YOU BABY PUSSY CUNT. YOU SWISH FAGGOT! PATHETIC BALLLESS SLUT WHORE WIMPY FLEA PRICK!

*(undergoes a metamorphosis and **TERRENCE** emerges)*

TERRENCE. *(frightened)* Why are you yelling? I didn't do anything? Why do you show up?

KENT. BECAUSE YOU CAN'T TAKE FUCKING CONTROL OF YOUR FUCKING WOMEN THAT'S FUCKING WHY I SHOW UP! BECAUSE YOU'RE ONLY HALF A FUCKING MAN THAT'S WHY I SHOW UP. WHAT THE FUCK DO YOU HAVE TO SAY ABOUT THAT FUCKING MENTAL FUCKING MIDGET? WHAT DO YOU HAVE TO SAY ABOUT BEING HALF A MAN? TERRENCE? DON'T MAKE ME ASK YOU TEN FUCKING TIMES. YOU THINK I'M IDA? YOU THINK I'M GONNA ASK YOU THE SAME THING TEN FUCKING TIMES? TERRENCE? GODDAMMIT. YOU HEAR I'M NOT ASKING TEN TIMES?

TERRENCE. Yes.

KENT. THEN DON'T MAKE ME FUCKING YELL AT YOU? TERRENCE, YOU HEAR ME? DON'T MAKE ME YELL AT YOU. ARE YOU? ARE YOU GOING TO MAKE ME FUCKING YELL AT YOU?

(as though to a child)

I said are you going to make me fucking yell at you!

TERRENCE. No.

KENT. Because I want to talk to you about Ida, about what happened with Ida. SHE ATTACKED ME!

TERRENCE. She doesn't like you.

KENT. SHE HATES MEN! THAT'S WHY!

(pause)

Terrence? She doesn't like men, does she?

(beat)

Terrence?

(pause)

COME FUCKING OUT AND TALK. TERRENCE?

*(jerks his body to force **TERRENCE** out)*

Where are you? I know you hear me. Terrence? Don't run away. Don't hide. I need to talk to you.

(violent body movements)

Terrence! You cunt! You pussy! Terrence!

Scene 9

(A Bench. Courthouse patio. **IDA** *is in her nurse uniform.* **MONNIE** *wears a court ID tag.* **IDA** *fishes with chopsticks at the noodles in the container of Chinese take-out.)*

IDA. There's a personality clash. You had one with Terrence, didn't you?

MONNIE. I tried with Terrence. I didn't bounce him off the wall, did I?

IDA. Well, I tried with Kent.

MONNIE. You didn't give him a chance, though, did you?

*(****IDA**** ignores her.* **MONNIE** *suddenly grabs* **IDA** *by the hair. A brief, almost motionless tableau.)*

IDA. Monnie. Monnie.

*(****IDA**** slowly moves and grabs* **MONNIE***'s hair.* **MONNIE** *lets go.)*

MONNIE. I was willing with Terrence, you know. I tried. I don't like a man that's just a lump of salt, but I didn't grab and shake him, did I? I looked for something to talk about.

IDA. Kent's a penis with a mouth telling me what I need!

MONNIE. He has very strong masculine instincts.

IDA. He was bragging about animal sex. I don't want animal sex from a man.

MONNIE. He's an aggressive dog. It's his aggressive personality. I told you.

IDA. I know you're upset he said he would drag me in the bushes.

MONNIE. I'm not upset about that.

IDA. I can see it.

MONNIE. I'm not upset about his saying it.

IDA. Uh-huh, yeah.

MONNIE. It's just his instinct talking.

IDA. See how far it got him.

MONNIE. I'm upset you beat him up!

(*beat*)

You can't blame Kent for who he is. Same as you can't blame Terrence for lying there. They can't help it. There's different style men in our lives, Ida.

IDA. I don't want to fight over it.

MONNIE. I don't either. They're not worth it in the long run, to argue over, because they come and go. We're always here. We've always each other.

IDA. (*indicates food*) You want the last bit?

MONNIE. No.

IDA. You sure?

MONNIE. Go ahead. It's good, though, thanks.

IDA. We like the same identical things except not the identical same style sex.

MONNIE. I know what you wanted for me with Terrence. It was really nice of you, really, really nice, really thoughtful, but it didn't work out. A man can't be everything.

IDA. I thought you were unhappy. I thought it might be fun for you.

MONNIE. It was really thoughtful, really, really nice. But now there's Kent, though, so it worked out almost the same.

IDA. I can try harder to get along with him, I guess. When we get together they can see we've made our choices, though, and we're sticking to them.

MONNIE. We just have to sit them down and let them know what we expect.

IDA. Ok.

MONNIE. I'll bring Kent over so we can.

IDA. I'll make sure Terrence doesn't run away.

MONNIE. They're competitive like men are with each other, and that's what it's all about with them.

IDA. Twins have a lot more pressure.

MONNIE. No wonder their personalities ran off in two directions.

IDA. What better way for me than for Terrence to be eleven.

MONNIE. And for Kent to be a macho man.

IDA. I love you.

MONNIE. I love you too.

IDA. There's no situation we can't handle if we work together.

(They embrace.)

Scene 10

(IDA's apartment. TERRENCE is in his underwear, pacing nervously.)

TERRENCE. I...I...no...I...I...

IDA. *(off-stage)* It's going to be OK.

TERRENCE. I... I...

(Toilet flushes.)

IDA. *(off stage)* Calm down. He's not coming tonight, is he, so don't worry.

TERRENCE. But. .. but...

(IDA enters in a slip.)

IDA. Calm down. He's not coming tonight, I said. You lie down like Ida told you. Terrence, you lie down like Ida told you.

(She grabs him and pulls him to the bed.)

TERRENCE. I...I don't want to.

IDA. Lie down now. Time to lie down and I'll make it all better. Lie down and be still. Don't move. Be still and don't move. Do what Ida says. She's going to take care of you. That's right, be still and listen to Ida. Listen to Ida, Terrence. She'll take care of you. She'll make you feel all better. I wonder what she can do to help?

(She exposes a breast.)

Look at what she has. Terrence, look what Ida has. Kiss and suck on Ida. Kiss and lick and suck on Ida and feel better. Come on. I said come on, Terrence. Suck on Ida.

(more commanding)

Suck on Ida.

(She moves her breast to his mouth)

That's right. That's good. That's right. Suck on Ida. Let Ida comfort you. Suck, suck, suck on Ida. Good, good, that's better. Tell Ida what happened. All about what happened. Was it at Disneyland? Did something happen on your birthday at Disneyland?

TERRENCE. Yes.

IDA. You got frightened at Disneyland?

TERRENCE. In the cup ride.

IDA. The pink and blue tea cups at Disneyland?

TERRENCE. Yes.

IDA. It's Ok. Suck on Ida. Don't be afraid. That feels good. That feels good when you suck on Ida. The tea cups frightened you?

TERRENCE. I was left.

IDA. Left alone?

TERRENCE. Yes.

IDA. It's OK now.

TERRENCE. On the tea cups.

IDA. Suck on Ida. It's OK. Suck on Ida. And you can tell me all about it.

TERRENCE. He made fun of me.

IDA. Suck. You were alone and afraid in a tea cup at Disneyland and Kent made you feel bad. But it's OK now, you see, because we'll tell him to respect you. We'll make it all better.

TERRENCE. He won't listen.

IDA. Sure he will. He'll listen. Now something else. Lie still. That's right. Lie still.

(She climbs over him and lowers her breasts down over his face.)

Here you are. Here you go. Now this one. Not hard. You hear! Not hard! That's right. This one now. Suck, suck, suck on this one. Then Ida has other things. Other things to do to you.

Scene 11

(MONNIE's apt. The stage is black.)

MONNIE. I still want you to take charge though.

KENT. *(off stage)* Don't worry your sweet titties about that, luv. Your egg and butter man is here.

(Monnie lights a candle. She's in a peignoir.)

MONNIE. I want it romantic but I want to be in your strong hands.

(Toilet flushes.)

KENT. *(off stage)* Don't worry your sweet peach, luv. The egg and butter man's gonna take care of you.

(KENT enters in tiny black bikini briefs. He walks around admiring her.)

KENT. How nice.

MONNIE. Thank you.

KENT. You're a beautiful Rheinland maiden from the Rheinland, from Wagner's Das Rheingold. You know Wagner's ouvre? The operas? The Rheinmaidens? The goddesses. Look at you, a regular goddess yourself, aren't you? And men take them and claim them, you know?

MONNIE. That's what you're going to do to me, isn't it? Take me and claim me. Make me yours.

KENT. I have done, haven't I? I have done. That's what we want, though, is it, luv?

MONNIE. Whatever you want. That's what I want. You're the man. I want whatever you want.

KENT. Whatever I want, is it?

MONNIE. I hope I didn't spoil our evening by mentioning your brother and seeing him tomorrow night at Ida's. I know Ida's sorry for being mean. She gets frustated when a man takes charge.

KENT. All I could do to control myself from doing violence, almost forgot she's a woman. Well, she's more the lesbian, that's all. She's not you, is she? She hates men, doesn't she? You're not the lesbian she is, are you? You don't hate men, do you?

MONNIE. I love men. I love a man that can't help himself. That's driven by strong urges. A man that claims me. I just hope I haven't been too bad.

KENT. Maybe you have been a little naughty.

MONNIE. I just want you and Terrence to work things out so we can do things together. Ida and Terrence and you and I. Maybe go dancing tomorrow night at Roseland Ballroom. It's swing night. I love swing.

KENT. We're going to do that but now let me look at you. You know Brunnhilde, don't you luv? From Wagner, from the operas, the ring cycle, very famous, right?

MONNIE. I've heard of her, I think.

KENT. Of course, you have. You're my Brunnhilde then, aren't you? My Rheinland maiden. My goddess of the Ring.

MONNIE. OK. And you're my man?

KENT. I could be. I could be your Siegfried, couldn't I? Do you think, luv, that I could be him? Siegfried, your wild man, and you're my Rheinland Maiden? My Brunnhilde? You think so, luv, you're my big female mystery? There's always this mystery, this thing that has to be discovered, this thing that has to be solved, so the maiden can be his. Maybe he can't tell if she's real or not. Maybe she's a figment of his imagination.

(feels her)

You feel real.

MONNIE. I am. I'm real.

KENT. You feel real, alright.

MONNIE. I am real.

KENT. Yes.

MONNIE. I am.

KENT. You feel real here, too.

MONNIE. Yes.

KENT. And here.

MONNIE. Your hands are strong.

KENT. They are looking for something.

MONNIE. OK.

(He rubs her fanny.)

KENT. Is this your sweet spot?

MONNIE. I think so.

KENT. Naughty, Monnie.

MONNIE. I know.

KENT. You know that, don't you?

MONNIE. Yes.

KENT. You know about the sweet spot?

MONNIE. You have to teach me.

KENT. I'm gonna have to spank you on your sweet spot for being bad.

MONNIE. I thought you might have to.

KENT. You know why?

MONNIE. You're the man?

KENT. I'm the man.

MONNIE. I know.

(He slaps her lightly on the fanny.)

MONNIE. Oh!

KENT. Say yes for more, naughty Brunnhilde.

MONNIE. Ok.

KENT. More?

MONNIE. Yes.

(He slaps her lightly on her fanny.)

You might have to kiss it and make it better, huh? You might have to do that because I've been bad and you're the man. You might have to kiss it and make it better.

(after each slap, a yes)

Yes.

KENT. Brunnhilde.

MONNIE. Yes.

KENT. Brunnhilde.

MONNIE. Yes.

KENT. Brunnhilde.

MONNIE. You have to kiss and make it better because you're the man.

KENT. I'm going to have to.

(He lifts the rear of her peignoir to kiss her fanny.)

Ich bin der Mann!

MONNIE. Yes.

KENT. Ich bin der Mann!

(He disappears under her peignoir.)

MONNIE. Siegfried?

KENT. *(under the peignoir)* He goes into the cave disguised and takes the ring from Brunnhilde. You can imagine what happens next? What happens in the cave?

MONNIE. You show me, OK? Whatever you want? You'll show me?

KENT. Ich bin der Mann!

MONNIE. *(high note)* Ah!

Scene 12

(IDA's apt. IDA is dressed up. She's having a drink. Another sits on the table. TERRENCE is off stage.)

IDA. It's going to be fun, Terrence. You'll have fun. Kent will be impressed when he sees you dance, all dressed up in style. Monnie's coming by for a vodka. I have to run out and get another bottle. Down at Bogie's Liquor, just down the block.

(louder)

I want to see how you look first. Before I go for the vodka. Are you about finished? I hope it all fits. The waist is alright isn't it? Do the pants fit at the waist? Terrence? Is the waist OK, not too tight? Is it? Terrence? Is the waist OK.

TERRENCE. *(off)* Yes.

IDA. Not too loose, though, is it? Not too big?

TERRENCE. *(off)* No.

IDA. And the length? The length of the trousers? I don't like excessive drape. Is the length OK?

TERRENCE. *(off)* Yes.

IDA. How about the shirt? The sleeves? They're not too short are they?

TERRENCE. *(off)* No.

IDA. But they're not too long are they? Terrence, are they too long? Because that wouldn't do, would it? The sleeves, Terrence, are the sleeves too long?!

(pause) Well...?

TERRENCE. *(off)* No.

IDA. The neck should be OK. I'm not too worried about the neck.

(beat)

But is it? Is it? Terrence, is it?

TERRENCE. *(off)* What?

IDA. *(impatiently)* Is the neck a fit?

TERRENCE. *(off)* Yes.

IDA. So, it all fits? Terrence? The shirt and trousers? It all fits OK?

TERRENCE. *(off)* Yes.

IDA. *(pause)* I don't know why you're being so private. It's not that I haven't seen the goods. You're like a little boy.

(pause)

Well...

(pause; half to herself)

Want to create an impression, don't you? Create a stir? You are such a little boy. More like a teenager, though, I think, a spoiled teenager.

(louder)

Hurry up though because I want to go out and get the good vodka because we're almost out! Terrence? Hurry because I want to run to Bogie's and get the Polish vodka Monnie likes.

(TERRENCE *enters in new, colorful, shirt and trousers.)*

That's very good. Very nice. Turn around a bit. Yes. What a cute little butt. Makes me want to give it a little paddle. Oh, yeah, the color suits you. You like them, don't you? I like them. But do you? What do you think? They give you a new feeling about yourself? You like them, don't you? Terrence?

TERRENCE. Yeah. They're alright. Good colors.

IDA. OK. I'm going to Bogie's for the vodka. Let Monnie in if she shows while I'm out. I won't be long. She said Kent's coming later. It'll be good you finally see him. Don't worry I'll be here. He'll mind himself. Don't worry about that. Very impressive, the way you look. You're OK? Right, Terrence? You're OK seeing Kent? You remember what we talked about? How it's all gonna be OK? You remember don't you?

TERRENCE. Yeah.

IDA. OK. Have your drink. I'll be right back.

(She hands him the drink.)

My pussy "dats" got brand new fur.

*(**IDA** rubs his crotch)*

My handsome pussy "dat."

*(**IDA** exits.)*

KENT. She'd piss her knickers, she knew whose cock she was stroking. And ain't you a Boy George in your flash drag, a sissy drink in your hand? What a wanker. Pussy is right.

(looking disdainfully at the vodka tonic in his hand.)

I'm not drinking this Polish piss.

(as the glass moves upward)

I'm not having a fucking Vodka Nellie Tonic, am I?

TERRENCE. I like it.

KENT. Well, I fucking don't.

(The drink is thrown across the room.)

TERRENCE. You're not taking over.

KENT. I'm not wearing these fucking clothes either!

TERRENCE. Ida bought them for me!

KENT. *(from one side of the face)* I don't like them.

TERRENCE. *(from the other side)* I do.

*(**KENT** struggles to take off the shirt.)*

KENT. I'll wear my fucking leather jacket and my fucking boots!

TERRENCE. These clothes are mine.

KENT. Pussy, pussy, pussy dat!

TERRENCE. Leave me alone. You fucking bully!

KENT. Oh, have we grown balls? We've balls now?

TERRENCE. Stop.

KENT. Let me feel. Let me see if you've grown balls.

TERRENCE. I have balls.

KENT. Where are they?

*(**KENT** gets a hand down around **TERRENCE**'s genitals.)*

You call these tiny marbles balls?

TERRENCE. I have balls.

KENT. These little raisins? No. These are balls. My balls. Feel these. These are a real man's balls.

*(**KENT** forces **TERRENCE**s trembling hand to his genitals.)*

These aren't little marbles, Terrence. Feel. These are huge. These are real balls. My balls.

(The intercom buzzes.)

That'll be my Monnie.

TERRENCE. No!

*(**KENT** tries to get to the intercom and **TERRENCE** tries to keep him away from it.)*

KENT. You'll learn how a man and woman go about it.

TERRENCE. We can't.

KENT. Then hide like you usually fucking do. Hide and watch a real man handle a woman.

TERRENCE. No.

KENT. Go hide like the baby you are! Hide.

*(**KENT** finally reaches the intercom button.)*

Is that you, luv?

*(Lights up downstairs on **MONNIE**, all dolled up.)*

MONNIE. Kent?

TERRENCE. Go away, Monnie!

MONNIE. Terrence?

TERRENCE. Go away!

KENT. *(**KENT** pulls **TERRENCE** away)* Fucking baby. Fucking little boy!

(fights a heavy hand to the buzzer)

Come on up, luv.

(MONNIE *starts up the stairs as the lights on her fade out.*)

TERRENCE. I want you to leave!

KENT. Fuck off!

TERRENCE. I'm not hiding!

KENT. You always do!

TERRENCE. Not this time!

(*There's knocking at the door.*)

KENT. Get lost!

TERRENCE. Don't let her in!

KENT. Retard!

TERRENCE. She doesn't like me!

KENT. Paranoid fucking baby!

(*Knocking at the door.*)

MONNIE (*off stage*) Kent, it's Monnie!

KENT. Right there, luv!

TERRENCE. Kent isn't here!

(*Knocking.*)

MONNIE. (*off stage*) Terrence? Open the door!

KENT. You can't win!

TERRENCE. Please, don't!

MONNIE. (*off stage*) What's going on in there?!

KENT. Nothing, luv.

TERRENCE. They'll find out.

(**KENT** *manages to open the door.* **MONNIE** *enters.*)

MONNIE. (*uncertain*) Kent?

TERRENCE. (*with great difficulty, trying to establish his personality*) I'm…I'm…I…

MONNIE. Terrence?

TERRENCE. (*anguishing*) I…I…I…

MONNIE. Where's Kent, Terrence?

TERRENCE. *(almost immobilized)* I...I...

KENT. *(suddenly* **KENT** *dominates)* I'm bloody Kent! I'm Kent! You can't tell I'm fucking Kent?!

MONNIE. I'm bound to be confused until you express yourself!

KENT. *(fights off* **TERRENCE** *who tries to emerge)* I...I...Mumph. Mumph. Mmmm...

MONNIE. Where's Ida?

KENT. She stepped out for some good vodka, Luv.

(MONNIE holds up a bottle of Polish Vodka.)

MONNIE. And look what I've brought. Well, won't go to waste, that's certain.

KENT. *(fighting the emerging personality of Terrence)* Mmmm... I...mmmm...

MONNIE. Sounded to me like you and Terrence were fighting. He's not in the back all upset is he? Is Terrence in the back upset at something you've said?

KENT. *(fighting)* Mmmm...mumm...mummm I'mmmm...

MONNIE. What is it? You didn't hurt his feelings did you?

KENT. *(struggling)* I'mmmmmm...!

(MONNIE moves toward the bathroom.)

MONNIE. Terrence? Terrence, are you in there? Terrence come on out? Terrence, come on out.

TERRENCE. *(fighting to emerge)* I..I...I...I...I...I

(MONNIE looks on in great confusion.)

TERRENCE. I...I AM TERRENCE.

KENT. *(emerging)* You twit. You fucking twit.

TERRENCE. *(asserting himself, tantrum)* I AM TERRENCE. I AM TERRENCE. I AM...MMMMM...

KENT. *(trying to emerge)* MUM...mmmm...It's Kent here, luv!

TERRENCE. I'm Terrence.

(IDA enters.)

IDA. Is everyone here?

*(**TERRENCE** and **KENT** contort as they fight for control.)*

MONNIE. Oh, my God.

IDA. What's going on?

MONNIE. He's two people.

KENT. *(to his inner **TERRENCE**)* I'm here and I am fucking staying.

TERRENCE. *(fighting back)* I don't want you here.

KENT. You can hide.

TERRENCE. Go away!

KENT. I'm staying.

TERRENCE. I want a life.

KENT. *(to **MONNIE**)* I find a woman who wants a real fucking man, and he drags me down with his wimpy fucking helpless self.

TERRENCE. *(to **IDA**)* He laughs at me because I don't have big balls like his.

KENT. You never fucking will!

(They strangle each other.)

IDA. Stop it! Both of you!

(She grabs them.)

TERRENCE. It's me, Terrence!

KENT. You pussy!

*(**KENT** smacks **TERRENCE**.)*

TERRENCE. Ida! Help!

IDA. Stop it! Let him go!

*(**IDA** smacks **KENT**.)*

KENT. Monnie! Help me!

*(**MONNIE** grabs **IDA**.)*

MONNIE. Don't hit Kent!

TERRENCE. Ida, it's me.

KENT. No, it's me.
IDA. Hold them down.

(The couples contort and roll.)

TERRENCE. It's me!
KENT. Me!
IDA. Grab them. Hold them.

(They are all entwined on the bed.)

MONNIE. Ah! Ah! Ah!
TERRENCE/KENT. Me. Me. Me. Me. Me. Me. Me.
IDA. Shut up!

(Ida silences him with a hand over the mouth. Blackout!)

Scene 13

(Moments later. "He" is gagged and bound. **IDA** *holds* **MONNIE***, comforting her.)*

MONNIE. I want Kent back. He's everything I ever wanted –

IDA. I know –

MONNIE. – and now I can't have him.

IDA. I wasn't done with Terrence either, was I? There's nothing we can't do, remember, Monnie? If we put our mind to it.

MONNIE. It isn't fair.

IDA. Listen to Ida. Ida has an idea. Are you ready to listen to Ida?

MONNIE. Yes.

IDA. We're rebels, right?

MONNIE. Rebels?

IDA. Yes. Deep down we're rebels.

MONNIE. We are?

IDA. Of course we are and there's nothing we can't do. Remember what we said about twins? About the cell dividing? Well, I believe they are both here. Terrence and Kent. The egg just didn't divide enough, but they are here. I'm gonna try to talk to Terrence. I'm gonna tell him what we want. Like we said we were. I'm going to ask him if he and his brother can behave themselves like we want them to and stay out of each other's business.

MONNIE. *(hopefully)* Ok.

IDA. Terrence? Terrence, I want to talk to you now. Ok?

(louder)

Terrence, I want to talk to you now! You understand?

TERRENCE. *(nods; muffled)* Mmmm hmmm.

*(***IDA*** removes the gag.)*

TERRENCE. Hi.

IDA. You understand that I like you?

TERRENCE. Yes.

IDA. I like you and Monnie likes Kent. She's gonna have a talk to Kent, too. She's gonna tell him that she doesn't want him popping out of you whenever he fucking pleases and causing trouble. But you have to try hard, too. You can't interfere when they're together, either. You can't decide to show up and just lie down like you do for me. You both have to follow the rules, or you have to leave. You understand, don't you, Terrence? You understand what we want to try? Do you Terrence? Do you understand?

TERRENCE. I'll try.

IDA. OK. Monnie wants to talk to Kent now.

   (to MONNIE)

   Go on, tell him what you want.

MONNIE. Kent? It's Monnie, Kent. Can I talk to you?

KENT. What's on your mind, luv?

MONNIE. I'd like to keep seeing you. I really want to make it work because Brunnehilde will miss her Siegfried. Do you understand how Brunnehilde will miss him? Do you Kent?

KENT. I'll only pop up for you then.

IDA. Tell him they better talk it over.

MONNIE. Maybe you and Terrence can have a little discussion among yourselves.

IDA. Make sure they have an understanding, and that they both agree to what we're saying.

MONNIE. You need to come to an understanding with your brother or it won't work out for us.

KENT. I'll do my best to get through to the little boy. It'd help if you undid me hands.

   (MONNIE unties him.)

MONNIE. We'll be right here just in case you need us, if you want to ask us anything.

(MONNIE *and* IDA *move aside.*)

KENT. (*stubbornly antagonistic*) Make my life fucking easier not to see you again.

TERRENCE. (*stubbornly antagonistic*) You're the problem!

KENT. Not so fucking loud.

TERRENCE. I don't trust you!

MONNIE. Everything OK, Kent, honey?

KENT. Fine, luv?

IDA. Terrence, you, too?

TERRENCE. Yes!

KENT. Keep out of my way.

(TERRENCE *grabs* KENT'*s testicles and squeezes.*)

TERRENCE. You keep out of mine.

KENT. Oh, you're grabbing balls now are you?

(*The discomfort causes them to stand.*)

MONNIE. Kent, are you reaching an agreement then?

KENT. (*over his shoulder*) That's right. Give us a moment. Why don't we have a little music.

(*to* TERRENCE)

Control yourself or they'll kick us out won't they?

TERRENCE. Let go.

KENT. You first.

IDA. Terrence? You've reached an understanding? Terrence? I'm asking if you've reached an understanding.

KENT. You fucking heard her.

TERRENCE. Yes.

MONNIE. Kent, you're in agreement with your brother?

KENT. That's right. No problem!

IDA. We'll have some music then. OK? Terrence? Maybe we'll have some music. Have our little party?

TERRENCE. Yes.

IDA. Do a little swing?

MONNIE. Kent? Are you ready for the party?

KENT. Getting there. Almost. Yes.

(**IDA** *crosses to the CD player.* **TERRENCE** *and* **KENT** *move distortedly.*)

TERRENCE. Let go.

KENT. You're the one holding on.

(*Swing plays.* **MONNIE** *misreads their movement as dancing.*)

MONNIE. Oh. looks like someone's ready to dance. Someone's ready to swing?

KENT. That's right. Kent's ready for his Monnie!

IDA. Terrence! You ready to swing?! Terrence!!!

(*loudly*)

I said, are you ready to swing!?

TERRENCE. Yes! I'm ready! I'm ready to swing!

(**TERRENCE** *breaks free and looks about for* **KENT.**)

MONNIE. Everyone's ready then! I'll get the drinks!

KENT. (*from one side of he face*) Don't worry. I'm still here, my brother, waiting my turn.

IDA. Terrence, let's dance!

(*She leads him in a swing dance.* **MONNIE** *enters with vodka, ice, glasses on a tray. She watches the dancing, then cuts in.*)

MONNIE. Kent, lead.

(*They dance.* **IDA** *cuts in.*)

IDA. Terrence, follow.

(*They dance.* **MONNIE** *cuts in.*)

MONNIE. Kent, lead!

(*They dance.* **IDA** *cuts in to dance with* **MONNIE.**)

IDA. You follow!

MONNIE. You lead!

IDA. This is great.

MONNIE. This is swing.

(They all dance together.)

MONNIE/IDA. Lead. Follow. Lead. Follow.
KENT/TERRENCE. Yes. Yes. Yes.
ALL. Go. Go.
Swing. Swing.
We love swing.
Let's swing!

(They dance.)

IDA. *(to* **MONNIE***)* See? There's nothing we can't do. Nothing. If we put our minds to it.
ALL. We love swing. Swing, swing, swing – lets swing!

(They dance. Swing music gets louder, and louder.)

ALL. *(singing)*
Sing, sing, sing, sing,
Everybody's got to swing!

(Fade out.)

THE END

www.ingramcontent.com/pod-product-compliance
Lightning Source LLC
Chambersburg PA
CBHW070833300426
44111CB00014B/2540